Rat Care

The Complete Guide to Caring for and Keeping Rats as Pets

Tabitha Jones

ISBN: 9781799047308

Rat Care

CONTENTS

INTRODUCTION

Before purchasing any pet it is important to understand that as a pet owner you are responsible for the care and wellbeing of your pet. It is important to try and learn as much as you can about the animal you are considering to keep as a pet to make sure that your lifestyle, household and financial status are suited to provide your pet with the best possible care. This guide has been designed to provide you with both precise and concise information about a chameleon's basic needs to help you provide your pet with the best quality care practices.

DESCRIPTION

Pet rats, also commonly known as 'Fancy Rats,' are a domesticated version of the common brown rat and are therefore part of the species known as '*Rattus Norvegicus*.' However household rats have been selectively bred for looks, color, size and temperament over the course of the last 100 years. They have been selectively bred to the point where there is almost no immediately obvious similarities between the household rat and their wild ancestors. Household pets are less aggressive towards humans and other rats due to the fact that they do not have to scrounge for food and defend territory. Rats make clean, intelligent and affectionate animals which show a similar level of loyalty to a household dog. Due to their intelligence and loyalty they have been anecdotally referred to as 'low-maintenance dogs.' However despite this nickname rats are relatively high maintenance in comparison to other common pet rodents – such as mice and ferrets.

Natural Habitat

Wild rats are opportunistic survivors and will therefore often live near human settlements to scavenge for food. Rats are also known to be both a terrestrial and an arboreal species. Due to the previous two reasons rats therefore can flourish in a wide range of habitats such as in human sewers, in houses, in clumps or vegetation or up trees. 1

Lifespan

Household pet rats normally live for between 2 and 3 years. Before committing to purchasing a pet rat it is important to make sure that you will be able to provide your rat with care for the entirety for its life. It is not uncommon for the general public to act squeamishly around rats which can make it difficult to find people to look after your pet if you go on holiday or will be absent for a few days. It is best practice to try and line up at least 3 people who would be willing to care for your pet rats while you are away before even purchasing them as pets. Some pet care stores provide a care service for owners while they are on holiday so it is also advisable to ask your local pet store if they offer this service.

Color Morphs

A key difference between wild rats and domesticated rats is their coloring. Wild rats are almost always a dull earthy brown color as it allows for the best camouflage in their natural habitat. Fancy rats, on the other hand, come in a wide variety of colors that range from white to cinnamon and ever blue grey!

Other Key Difference Between Wild Rats and Domesticated Rats

There is a big difference in body structure between wild rats and Fancy rats. Wild rats have larger bodies than fancy rats as it helps them survive in the wild. Despite having smaller bodies than their wild counterparts, Fancy rats have larger ears and longer tails as these physical traits have been deemed to be aesthetically pleasing and have therefore been exaggerated through selective breeding. The main other difference between Fancy rats and their undomesticated counterpart is their behavior. Fancy rats are tamer, more comfortable around humans, have a better tolerance to overcrowding (which can be experienced during the breeding process or in pet shops) and have far less caution in trying new foods than wild rats would. Domesticated rats are also vastly less frightened of unexpected lights and sounds which is probably due to their safe environment and close proximity to human life. Domesticated rats also tend to fight for longer periods of time where as a wild rat will flee as soon as they feel a fight is unwinnable. The differences in behavioral traits between wild and Fancy rats is theorized to be a down to the dramatic difference in environment rather than a genetic difference.

Size

Both wild rats and Fancy rats come in a plethora of different sizes. Most rats will have a body of anywhere between 6 inches and 12 inches. Males are normally larger than females and, as previously mentioned, wild rats are usually larger than rats bred in captivity.

Differences Between the Sexes

Male rats are called 'Bucks' and female rats are called 'Does.' It is very easy to tell the difference between the sexes as male rats have prominent and visible testicles which are located underneath their tails. These testicles become visible at a young age and well in advance of when the rat would leave its mother. The only time when a male's testicles are not visible is when they are scared or feel threatened as they draw their testicles inside their bodies to protect them. The breeder or employee in the pet store should be able to easily identify the sex of a baby rat - if they are unable to do this it is best practice to not purchase a rat from that location. Both male and female rats make great companions but there are some important differences between the sexes that should be considered before purchase. Does are generally smaller, more agile and active than Bucks. Does also have a smoother, or less curly if they are rexes, coat. Does are also less likely to smell due to the fact that they do not scent mark their habitats. It is important to note that Does will also become in heat every 5 days or so and the process will last for around 12 hours. During this period your Doe will become dramatically more skittish and it is therefore best practice to not handle her during this process. Bucks are generally larger and more docile than Does. Bucks tend to be lazier than Does and are much more likely to curl up on your lap. It is important to remember that a Buck is highly likely to scent mark you during any handling session - a scent mark consists of a few drops of urine.

RATS AS PETS

The practice of keeping rats as pets is a fairly new phenomenon that has occurred over the last 100 years or so. Pet rats are affectionate, docile and intelligent pets that appear to enjoy human company. Compared to other small pets, rats are relatively easy to care for and are therefore a great addition to any family. Despite being easy to care for it is still important to remember that as their care giver you are responsible for their health, happiness, housing, food, warmth and entertainment.

Transporting your Rat

It is best practice to not transport your rat unless it is absolutely necessary - for example for trips to the vet and when you first purchase your rat. It is important to try and minimize your pet's stress during the transportation process. The first way to reduce your rat's stress is to provide your rat with a suitable and secure cage with fresh bedding material. It is best practice to provide your rat with a cage it is already familiar with and also has a hide within it. It is important to provide your pet rat with both food and water during the journey. Food can be supplied in pellet form and water can be provided in the form of apples, pears or watery potatoes – however a water bottle will be needed for longer trips to provide your rat with proper hydration. It is important to cover the cage and keep it dark while also keeping decent air ventilation. During the journey it is best practice to keep the car as quiet as possible as loud and unfamiliar sounds can cause your pet stress. The final method of reducing your pet's stress is to plan your route in advance to try and minimize time in transit.

Intelligence

It is not common knowledge but rats are of a similar level of intelligence to dogs and have been given the nickname of 'low maintenance dogs.' Like dogs, rats become very attached to their owners and display similar levels of loyalty and affection. Due to their high level of intelligence rats are fairly high maintenance in comparison to other pet rodents. It is important to allow your pet rat to have at least an hour of time outside of its cage every day. Rats are highly inquisitive and will become depressed or stressed if they are not given enough attention or enough environmental stimulation.

Handling

It is important to purchase rats that have been

handled from a young age as they will already be accustomed and receptive to human contact. The best practice for picking up a rat is to place one hand gently underneath its chest and behind its forelegs and use your free hand to support the rats hind legs. It is important to not squeeze your rat too tightly as this can cause serious internal injuries - it is therefore important to supervise any small children who are handling your rats. It is imperative to **NEVER** pick your rat up by its tail as this **WILL** injury your pet. A good method to allow your rat to become more accustomed to being in contact with you is to carry it around in a jumper pocket - this will allow your rat to get used to your scent and body warmth. As previously mentioned rats are highly intelligent and can therefore learn a plethora of tricks. If you are hoping to train your rat it is important to regularly handle it to improve how receptive your rat is during the training process. There will be an in-depth section on training later in this manual.

Risk of Cancer

Sadly, cancer is a common problem in pet rats and can dramatically shorten their life span. Although not every rat will develop cancerous tumors it is important to be aware of the risk before purchasing a pet rat. Unspayed female rats have the highest risk of developing cancer. Tumors can be dealt with if spotted early - however the price of surgery is not cheap. It is important to consider if you can afford the surgery or if you would be able to euthanize a pet rat, that has developed cancer, to prevent it from suffering.

Selecting a Rat For Purchase

When selecting your rat for purchase it is always best practice to actually view the rat in person to check for any obvious signs of ill health. The rat should appear alert during your viewing. If possible it is best to try and see the rat feed as this will give you a good idea of the rat's eating habits and if it has any issues during feeding. It is best practice to purchase captively bred rats rather than wild-caught rats due to the wide availability of rats bred in captivity. Buying captively bred rats likewise lowers the chance of genetic problem or illnesses.

Recording

It is highly advisable to keep a record throughout your rat's life. By regularly noting down weight, length and feeding patterns you will have a useful resource to help notice any potential problems with your pet rat and to likewise make sure it is in good health. It is also important to check your pet rats for lumps on a regular basis and to track if they grow or not. This helps to spot cancer in your rat at an early stage which gives your pet a higher chance of survival.

Food

Rats are omnivores and appreciate a varied diet. It is possible to buy specialized rat food pellets and food blocks from pet stores but they can easily be fed on a diet of brown rice, vegetables and dried protein sources such as dog food. While rats will appreciate scraps from your dinner it is important to not allow your rat to become overweight as this will have a negative impact on their life. Fruit, sunflower seeds and peanuts seem to be highly preferred food but can cause skin problems so should be only given to your pet as a treat. It is best practice to provide your rats with a dish full of food each day and to allow them to eat what and when they want.

Water

It is important to provide your rats with clean and fresh water at all times. The usual sipper bottles sold in pet stores for rodents are perfect. It is considered best practice to have more than one sipper bottle to hand as your pet may gnaw through the plastic.

A Note on Breeding

We do not recommend that you breed your pet rats and will therefore not be discussing the breeding process in this care manual. This manual is aimed at providing you with the information you need to make your pet rats happy and healthy. Does will normally have between 8 and 14 kittens per litter, but it is not uncommon for a doe to have over 20 kittens in a litter. I believe it is in the best interest of both the owners and animals to provide information about breeding rats in a general care manual. If you are determined to become a breeder we advise that you contact your local Rat Club and ask for contact details for a local breeder who may be able to provide you with a specialized course in breeding.

WHERE TO PURCHASE YOUR RATS

Before you purchase a rat from any location it is important to consider whether the establishment meets the following standards. Firstly it is important to make sure that the establishment socializes their rats properly. It is likewise important that they allow the mother rat to rest between litters and that both parent rats are healthy and genetically sound animals. It is important to not purchase rats that are under 5 or 6 weeks old – if the establishment of purchase is not able to give you the rats date of birth you should not purchase your pet from that location. It is important to watch the rats be handled before you purchase them to make sure they are accustomed to human contact as they should have been handled often during their lives. Lastly, any location that you purchase a pet rat from should question you about your housing for the rats. If they do not show interest in how you will care for the rats after purchase it indicates that they have little interest in the rats welfare.

Breeders

It is considered best practice to purchase your rats from a breeder. The main reason for this is that a breeder will only have a few litters of baby rats (interestingly called 'kittens') at a time and will therefore be able to provided them with better quality care and handling time. Rats bought from breeders generally live for longer as they do not experience the stress of transportation and living in a busy, and noisy, shop at an early age. Purchasing rats from a breeder also allows you to meet the rats parents and to therefore check that they are happy, healthy and friendly. It is possible to find a responsible breeder by contacting your local/national rat club as many clubs will keep a 'Kitten Register' which indicates the best breeders.

Pet Shops

Purchasing rats from a pet shop is considered more of a gamble. The main reason for this is that it is impossible to know how caring and responsible each individual member of staff is which therefore means that the quality of the rats care is unknown. Advice and care given by pet shop staff is unreliable due to the fact that they do not necessarily need experience of a qualification to secure the job. It is important to ask where the pet shop gets their rats from. If they are sourcing their rats from local breeders or breeding a few litters themselves then this indicates that the rats are more likely to be of a higher quality. If your local pet shop purchase their rats at wholesale you should not purchase your rats from that location. Wholesale rats can suffer great stress due to the constant transportation and lack of individual care they experience. The last major problem with purchasing rats from a pet store is the fact that they have an increased chance of catching an illness or disease from the other animals in the store – which can shorten their lives.

Rat Rescue

Rescue organizations sometimes have rats that need a new home, and your national rat club will be able to put you in contact with members who deal with rescued rats. Rats that end up in rescue care normally come from either owners who have a breeding pair but were unable to keep up with the litters of babies or have been seized by animal welfare organizations. If you adopt an adult rat from a rescue you will have a good idea of its health and temperament. Getting a baby rat from a rescue is more of a gamble as their parents, health and temperament will be unknown. Rescuing a rat can be a very rewarding experience as you are taking an animal who may have had a hard life and are giving it a loving home. However we recommend that you do not rescue a rat until you have owned a few happy and healthy rats purchased from either a breeder or a pet store. Rescued rats may have special requirements to keep them happy and it is best to have experience with 'normal' rats beforehand.

CAN MULTIPLE RATS BE HOUSE TOGETHER?

In the wild rats naturally live in social groups and it is therefore not best practice to keep a single pet rat. If a rat is kept on its own it has a higher chance of developing cancer due to the stress it will feel due to its isolation. Regular handling is not a suitable substitute for the consistent company of another rat.

Best Practice for Housing Multiple Rats

If you are opting to buy multiple rats and house them together it is considered best practice to only house rats of a similar sex to avoid any unplanned breeding. It is likewise considered best practice to purchase rats that have been raised together as they already be comfortable with each other's company. It likewise lowers the chance of your new rats feeling stressed during both the transportation process and while they explore and adjust to their new environment. A further advantage of purchasing rats that are already comfortable with each other is the fact that you will not need to worry about introducing your unfamiliar rats. Male rats have a tendency to become aggressive as they are innately territorial.

How to Introduce Unfamiliar Rats

It is best practice to introduce rats to their new companions when they are young – preferably under 10 weeks in age. However, it is possible to introduce adult rats to each other. When introducing adult rats, it is important to first thoroughly clean the cage that houses the rats you currently keep. The cleaning process removes any territorial scents which simultaneously makes the new rat feel less intimidated and your current rats feel less defensive and aggressive. Even after the cage has been cleaned it is best practice to introduce the rats on neutral territory as your current rat may still see the cage as their territory. It is not uncommon for newly introduced rats to fight. If you are concerned about your rats fighting it is possible to introduced them multiple times on neutral territory to minimize the chance of them fighting. Introducing two adult male rats is especially difficult and it is recommenced to introduce them slowly over the course of about a week.

HOUSING YOUR RAT

Your rats will spend the majority of their lives in their cage, and as previously mentioned they are both intelligent and active creatures, it is therefore important to create a safe and stimulating environment for them to live in. It is considered best practice to place your rats cage in a busy location of your house to help keep them entertained and to avoid them feeling lonely.

Best type of Cage

The best type of housing for your pet rats is, unquestionably, a wire cage with a wooden floor. Wire cages provide your rat with good ventilation that prevents the buildup of harmful ammonia – due to rat droppings and urine. The ventilation also provides your rat with smells and sounds from your house which will interest, stimulate and entertain them. Wire cages also provide your rat with a source of entertainment as you can interact with your pet through the bars (by petting or feeding them) as well as giving your pet a place to climb. The wood flooring of the wire cage also helps your rat feel more secure due to its difference in coloring.

Other Types of Cages

A glass aquariums can be used to house your rats but has the downside of little, to no, air ventilation. As previously mentioned rat droppings and urine creates ammonia which is harmful to your rat. If you house your rat in an aquarium you will need to thoroughly clean your rats housing every few days to avoid the buildup of ammonia. Hamster cages are sometimes used to house baby rats but are unsuitable for adult rats as they tend to be too small. A decent alternative cage is a Perspex house – such as the Rotastak cage. These houses are designed to be interconnected with other units which allows you to create an interesting, and easily changeable, housing complex for your rat to explore.

Optimum size of a Rat Cage

You should house your rats in a cage that has a minimum of two square feet of floor space per rat. It is considered best practice to get taller cages as it gives your rats more space to explore. Unlike most other pets kept in cages, rats do not feel stressed by large spaces and you should therefore try to accommodate your rat in as large a cage as possible.

Cleaning

It is important to keep your rat cage clean as a poorly maintained enclosure can create health risks for your pet. Rat feces and soiled bedding should be cleaned and removed as soon as you spot it as it poses the highest risk of disease, parasites and ammonia buildup. It is best practice to clean your rat's cage at least once a week with a rodent-safe disinfectant and then to rinse the cage well. It is also possible to use a disposable wipe to clean the inside of your cage. It is also important to clean your hands before and after cleaning the cage and handling your rats to minimize the chance of infection between both yourself and your pet.

A Rat Toilet

Just like dogs, rats do not like to soil their sleeping and eating quarters. You can use this to your advantage by providing your rats with a toilet. Rat toilets are generally small and shallow plastic boxes with a wire roof to allow the feces and urine to slip through the bars. It is important to place the rat toilet in the opposite corner of the cage to where the food and water bowls are kept. This promotes the idea that the box is to be used for excretion purposes and most rats will work this out very quickly. It is common for rats to designate a corner of their cage for toilet purposes and it is therefore best practice to place the toilet in this corner. A rat toilet makes cleaning the cage a lot easier as most of the feces and urine will be concentrated in a singular area.

A Comfortable Nest

It is natural for rats to want to hide themselves during times of vulnerability – such as when they are asleep. It is therefore best practice to include a nest in your rat's cage to allow them to feel secure while they sleep. The two best options for a rats nest are: a plastic house or a wicker ball with an opening in it. The plastic house is a good choice because they are cheap, astatically pleasing, easy to clean and widely available from pet stores. A wicker ball on the other hand has the benefit of being a closer replication of what a rat would choose to sleep in in the wild.

Heating

It is important to place your rat cage in a space that will not experience dramatic changes in temperature. Rats should be kept at a temperature of between 65 and 75 degrees Fahrenheit. If it is an especially hot day you can provide your rats with a small shallow dish of cool water to play in. Similarly on especially cold days you can provide your rats with extra bedding to snuggle in. Both of these techniques allow your rats to adjust their surrounding depending on their body temperature needs.

Toys

As previously mentioned rats are highly intelligent animals. It is therefore best practice to provide your pet rats with multiple toys to play with. A good example of toys for rats are hammocks, places to hide, ping-pong balls, parrot ladders to climb, a wheel to run in (make sure it is large and solid), small stuffed toys and even toilet paper rolls to hide in and run through. Rats will entertain themselves and explore any new object placed into their cage so it is best practice to mix up their toys every once in a while. Providing your pet rats with toys is also a great way to entertain them if you spend long periods of time away from home. It is important to not place string or yarn in your rats cages as they have the potential to consume it and choke themselves. Use a mixture of common sense and creativity when providing toys for your pets – if you are ever unsure there are multiple ideas available online.

SUBSTRATES

The term Substrate is defined as being the surface or material on which an organism lives, grows or obtains its nourishment. In terms of Fancy rat care the substrate is what you choose to line your rat's cage. There are multiple different substrates available to use in your rat's cage.

Aspen Shavings

Aspen shavings are great for lining the floor of your rat cage. A great bonus is that they collect urine and faeces and can easily be scooped out with a dog or cat litter scoop.

Beech Chippings

Beech chippings are cheap and readily available from all reptile stores. They are not as absorbent as Aspen shavings and will likewise need to be removed once they are dirtied. However they come in three different grades – small, medium and large. This allows you to choose which grade best suits your rat.

Oatbran and Wheatbran

Although it sounds like a strange choice to line a rat

cage but both oatbran and wheatbran are a great and inexpensive choices. They a very similar aesthetic as wood chippings but have the benefit of being more easily digestible and dramatically cheaper than their wood chipping counterparts.

Newspaper and Paper Towels

Both newspaper and paper towels are easily obtained and inexpensive. They make decent flooring if your rat has an injury as they are smooth and do not have any potentially harmful edges. However there is the potential for harmful inks to be present within the paper which make them not ideal for long term use.

Substrates to Avoid

The following substrates should be avoided due to the fact that they are either toxic or indigestible: Cedar shavings, gravel, kitty litter, Redwood shavings, pesticides and fertilizer.

GROOMING

Rats are incredibly clean animals. They spend almost a third of their waking life grooming themselves! It is therefore it is rarely neceasiry to provide your rat with a bath. Light coated rats may need a bath to remove 'stains' from their coats if you wish to keep your rats looking as presentable as possible. However there are still aspects of grooming that are necessary to keep your rat happy and healthy.

Tail Grooming

It is not uncommon for rats to not properly clean their tails and can therefore develop dark stains on their tails. If left uncleaned for a long period of time your rats tail may develop a skin condition. To clean your rats tail it is best practice to gently rub it with a soft toothbrush coated in either an animal shampoo or bicarbonate of soda. Do not brush your rats tail too hard as this can potentially remove the skin from its tail which will cause your pet pain.

Nail Trimming

It is not imperative to cut your rats nails but some owners choose to do so. It is considered best practice to take your rat to the vet for the first time you have their nails cut so you can be taught the correct process of trimming. Rats have a 'quick' (a red vein inside their finger) that can be cut during the nail trimming process. Cutting the 'quick' is not fatal but is a painful experience. Most owners will provide their rats with a disinfected stone or brick in their cage to allow their rats to climb on while also naturally wearing down their nails.

Smell

It seems counter intuitive but leaving a small section of used bedding in your rats cage is a good way to stop your rats smelling. If you complete clean their cage and remove all traces of their familiar scent rats will begin to urinate at an increased rate to reaffirm their territory. This will therefore lead to both the cage and your rat smelling. A further way to stop your rat smelling is to occasionally provide them with a small dish of water to play in and clean themselves in.

TRAINING

As previously mentioned rats are the intellectual equals of dogs and can therefore be trained in a similar fashion. It also seems that rats enjoy being trained as both enjoy the human interaction of the training process and seem to enjoy 'pleasing' their owners. Training your rat is a perfect way to strengthen the bond between you and your pet as well as being a cool thing to show to non-rat owners.

The Key Components of Training

The following bullet points are the five most important aspects of training any animal:

- Trust
- Positive reinforcement
- Repetition
- Patience
- Consistency

Pre-requisites for successful training

It is vital that your rats are well socialized and accustomed to both your presence and being handled by you. It is not a good idea to try to train new rats immediately after purchasing them as they will not trust you and may be frightened or stressed by the training process. Younger rats are generally more adaptable to training and will therefore pick up new tricks at a faster rate. However younger rats will also have a shorter attention span which can make the process of training them a long process. Older rats, especially Bucks, will have a longer attention span but less willingness to do physical based training.

Preparation

Before starting to train your rat it is best to know how your rat enjoys spending it's time and what food it loves so you can reward it appropriately. It is important to find one or two healthy treats to reward your rat with and help them stay healthy and motivated during the training process. We recommend using the following treats as rewards: peas, sunflower seeds, banana chips and yogurt. The reason it is important to know your pet rat's preferences is to allow you to work with your pet's natural inclinations and to praise and positively re-enforce the behavior you want.

Training the First Trick

The first trick we recommend teaching your rat is to come on command. We recommend this trick because it is both easy to train and practical. The goal of this trick is to have your rat come to you whenever you make a certain noise, such as call its name, so they can be rewarded with a treat. It is best practice to start training this trick within the rat's cage and to choose a time when your rats are active. Choose a command noise or word and repeat it in a consistent and positive voice and have your treat of choice in your hand by the cage door. Once your rat approaches you reward it with the treat and some verbal praise and petting. Once your rat consistently comes to the cage door it is time to continue their training outside of the cage. Start at a close distance and repeat the process – if they seem reluctant to come to you across large distances move closer.

Advanced tricks

There are a plethora of tricks that Fancy rats can learn and are all taught in a similar method of patience and repetition. Some common tricks include:

- Jumping
- Standing
- Kissing
- Riding on your shoulder

What if the training is not working?

It is important that you go into the training process with the intention of having fun and bonding with your pet – any tricks your pet learns will be an added bonus! It is very uncommon for a rat to be untrainable. If the training is not working it is important to think about if you have a close relationship with the rat you are trying to train and if your rat is in the correct mind set to learn tricks. Rats can easily become bored or repeated training and may likewise be disinterested due to the time of day. Another reason for a rats disinterest may be that you are offering them the wrong type of treat as a reward. It is important to remember that rats, like dogs and even humans, learn at different rates and some rats will therefore take longer to train. If a rat seems impossible to train it is probably advisable to stop trying to train it and just enjoy playing with it and caring for it.

FINAL THOUGHTS

Thank you for purchasing our pet care manual on caring for a rat. We hope you have found the information both interesting and informative. We hope that this book has allowed you to make an informed choice on whether owning a chameleon suits you and if so we hope that the information will help you to provide the best quality care for your pet chameleon.

We will be publishing multiple other pet care manuals on our author page on Kindle. If you have an interest in exotic and exciting pets then we highly suggest you check out our other work.

I am passionate about providing the best quality information to our customers. We would highly appreciate any feedback, or reviews, you could leave us on our Kindle page to allow us to help create the best possible pet care products available on the market.

Made in the USA
Middletown, DE
04 December 2019